why "365 days after you"?

this title is more than a measure of time; it's a journey through the heart's seasons, a personal odyssey set in the days following a significant departure. under the moon's gentle glow, each 'after you' day represents a step into uncharted territory—a land where memories linger like morning mist, and the future unfolds with the uncertainty of a path not yet taken. these 365 days are not just about the absence of someone deeply loved and now gone; they're also about the presence of a new self waiting to be discovered in the wake of loss, cocooned in the warmth of a bed and blanket.

this book is a testament to the resilience of the human spirit, to the bitter-sweetness of moving on, and to the beauty of transformation that often follows the end of something once thought irreplaceable. it's about finding light in the darkest of places, like a beacon guiding lost birds, about learning to breathe again in a world that feels unfamiliar, savoring the aroma of coffee in the morning air, and about growing like a waterfall, cascading in ways you never thought possible. "365 days after you" is an invitation to walk with me through a year of healing, of reflection, of laughter and tears, of finding joy in the small things, and of learning to love the person who emerges from the other side of grief. so, as you turn these pages, remember: each day is a story, each emotion a brushstroke on the canvas of a year. and every ending, no matter how painful, is also the beginning of something new.

365

days

after

you

365 days
after you

- a collection for the romantic and broken souls

mr. den

before the first day dawned, before the first page turned, there was silence—the deep, echoing silence that comes after a door closes, after a story ends. this is not a tale of that silence, but of the life that fills the quiet after the storm.

this is a journey through 365 days—each day a step, each step a story, each story a lesson learned in the solitude of a heart relearning its beat. these pages hold the chronicle of a year lived in the shadow of absence and the light of personal growth.

in the following entries, i bare the intricate dance of my soul—a dance of loss, of love, of letting go, and of looking forward with courage. it's a dance we all know, each in our own way, set to the unique rhythm of our experiences.

so, before we begin, take a deep breath. hold it for a moment. feel its weight and its lightness all at once. now let it go. with it, release your expectations. let your *eyes scream* if they must, and *scrawl* your feelings in the *diary* of the heart. prepare to walk with me through the highs and the lows, the laughter and the tears, the pain and the sweetness of finding oneself again.

embrace the timing of this journey, where every word is scrawled with the essence of life, and let butterflies of anticipation flutter in your eyes.

welcome, dear reader, to day 1.

day 1

the world has stopped.
it's so weird now.
every time my phone beeps, i look at it really fast.
i always think it might be you. but it's not.

day 2

i keep asking myself,
can't we just stop being angry and distant?
can we start over?

it's a question
that keeps going round in my head.
i wish we could erase all the bad stuff
and go back to the good times.

i miss us,
the way we were before everything went wrong.
but i don't know if you feel the same.
are you thinking about this too?
or am i alone in wishing we could try again?

day 3

we said goodbye
and now
your words
keep playing
in my head

like a song
that won't stop

it hurts
every time

day 4

i can't eat.
food tastes like ash without you.

day 5

the emptiness is suffocating.

every corner of this house
whispers memories of you, of *us*.

day 6

today, i saw a couple holding hands, and it stirred something deep within me. it felt like the universe was playing with my emotions, showing me what we used to have.

their intertwined fingers triggered memories of us, a love that once defined our world. watching them share those tender moments, i couldn't help but feel a surge of emotions—a poignant reminder of the connection we once shared and the void that now exists. in that moment, the universe seemed to challenge the strength of my heart, urging me to find solace in the echoes of the 'us' that still resides in the recesses of my soul.

day 7

one week
without you
my heart feels empty
like something big is missing
the ache is always there
every minute
tells me
you're not here

day 8

your smell
still on your pillow
i hold it tight
hoping to keep
a piece of you

day 9

i went out
but everything has changed
colors are dull
sounds are soft
like the world is faded
since you left

day 10

i find myself talking to your shadow,
hoping it would talk back.

day 11

i wore your favorite shirt today.
it still smells like you.
is it strange that i find comfort in this?

day 12

the night feels longer without your messages.
i keep scrolling through our old chats,
searching for *a piece of you.*

day 13

tried to cook your favorite meal.
it didn't taste the same.
nothing does anymore.

day 14

i remember
you'd get mad
and throw an *"i hate you"* my way

my comeback was always
"i love you more"

those little fights
they were our thing
i miss that
i miss us

day 15

every knock on the door makes my heart race,
wishing it's *you*.
it never is.

day 16

last night when i could not sleep,
i remembered how we used to sleep on calls.

day 17

i saw someone wearing your perfume today.
for a moment,
it was as if you were there.

day 18

i dreamt of you last night.
in my dreams, you still loved me.
waking up was a *nightmare*.

day 19

today, i accidentally set a table for two.
old habits die hard.

day 20

i heard our song on the radio.
it felt like the universe was mocking my pain.
i cried again.

day 21

i tried to *delete* your number today but couldn't.

it's like erasing you from my phone
is erasing you from my life.

day 22

i was laughing thinking about a memory of us.
the laughter quickly turned into tears when i realized
you aren't mine anymore.

day 23

it rained.
the sky cried,
just like me.

the raindrops
tapping on my window
felt like they understood how i felt.

it was as if the sky could feel the same things
happening inside me.

day 24

went to our cafe. the barista asked about you.
i pretended not to hear.

day 25

i tried writing a text message to you,
but the words wouldn't come.

there's too much to say
and not enough words.

day 26

i'm learning
that feeling sad
isn't only about crying.

it's in the little things—
like cooking for myself
or sleeping on one side of the bed.

those everyday activities
remind me of what's missing,
and it makes everything feel a bit *lonelier*.

day 27

some days,
the weight of your absence is heavier.

today is one of those days.

day 28

i keep finding traces of you
in the smallest corners of my life.

today, it was a ticket stub
from our first movie date.

day 29

i spoke to a friend about you today.
it felt like betraying our memories,
but also like a step towards healing.

day 30

the world keeps moving,
but i'm stuck in the day you left.

it's a lonely place to be.

day 31

today,
i managed to go through the whole day
without crying.

it's a small victory, but i'll take it.

day 32

i've started to accept
that some days are better,
some are worse.

it's the dance of healing, i suppose.

day 33

i walked past your favorite bookstore.
i didn't go in. not yet. not ready.

day 34

do me a favor,
please come back

it is still not late, should i call you tonight?

day 35

ahh i still remember
the first time we confessed so many things;
it was 3 am.

should we start a convo again at 3?

day 36

and here i am again,
in the same place, yes, in my bed,
crying,
thinking about all those memories,
looking at all those pictures,
reading all those texts.

now that you're gone,
only this is my treasure,
and i'm gonna learn to live with this.

day 37

i smiled at a stranger today.
it felt good to connect, even in a small way.

day 38

i still talk to you in my head.
sometimes, i wonder if you hear me.

day 39

now it feels like you are away,
and it isn't bothering you.

is it true?

day 40

now that you are gone,
i am starting to change my playlist
slow and sad is my new taste

i miss you hun

day 41

found your note in a book

your writing
once so known
now feels like
a piece from
a past life

day 42

i saw couples everywhere today.
their happiness feels like
a language i once spoke fluently
but now
can barely understand.

day 43

i tried to wear a smile today.

but smiles, like bandaids,
can't cover the depth of a wound.

day 44

your mug broke today
the one you always used
it's silly but
it felt like a sign
that nothing sticks around forever

i'm guessing that goes for pain too
i sure hope it does

day 45

that song came on today
the one that was 'us'
now it's just notes
floating around
bringing back ghosts
of what we used to be
i'm trying hard
to let them go.

day 46

you're turning into a memory
and memories, they get fuzzy
they slip away
that thought
it's scary
because i don't want to forget
any piece of you

day 47

i sat in our park
the sun dipped low
its colors took me back
to your eyes
and i thought
maybe you're out there
under this same sky
watching the same sunset
without me

day 48

i laughed today, a real laugh.
then i cried because you weren't there to share it.

day 49

everyone keeps telling me
that this phase will pass,
and it is just a matter of time
before move on.

some of them even suggest
that i should start looking for someone else.

i don't know what's wrong with people!
why can't they understand
that i love you way too much

looking for someone else!
damn that's so crazy

day 50

halfway to a hundred days without you.

each day
is a step
away from you,

but also,
a step towards something new.

day 51

i whispered your name today,
and the wind carried it away.

maybe it's time for me to let go too.

day 52

the rain came down
just like my tears
it's like the whole sky
is sad with me
crying for a love
that's not here anymore

day 53

dreamt of you last night.

in my dream,
you were reaching out to me, but
as i got closer,
you faded away,
just out of reach.

day 54

i found myself talking to you in my head today,
asking *questions* i'll never get *answers* to.

it's a conversation that never ends.

day 55

walked past our spot today,
the one with the good fries.
memories hit me like a wave;
i could almost see us
sitting there,
laughing without a clue
that one day
it would all be just this—
memories without you.

day 56

your absence is like a cold shadow over my life.
some days it's all i can feel, a chill i can't escape.

day 57

still missing you
like it was day one

your absence is a shadow
that follows me
everywhere i go

i keep thinking
you'll come back
and turn this shadow
into light
but for now
i'm here
marking the days
without you

day 58

here's an ache in my chest that won't go away.
it's a constant reminder of
the empty space *you left behind*.

day 59

i realized i'm not just missing you;
i'm missing the person i was with you.

day 60

two months without you.
time is moving,
but i feel stuck in the moment you walked away.

day 61

tried to clear out some of your things.

each item is a chapter of our story,
and it hurts to close the book.

day 62

the mornings are the hardest
waking up to the space
where you used to be

i reach out
half expecting you'll be there
but it's just cold sheets
and the echo of an old routine

i get up
the day starts
but that empty space
it follows me

day 63

i saw a couple fighting and making up.

i envied them,
not for their fight,
but for their second chance
to fix things
to hold each other again
we won't get that
our story ended
without that sweet make-up moment

day 64

the world seems a bit duller without you.
colors aren't as bright,
laughter not as loud.

i'm living in a muted version of life.

day 65

i wonder if you think of me.
do i ever cross your mind,
or am i just a ghost of your past?

day 66

i tried to write about you today.
my pen was heavy, the words heavier.
each sentence was a teardrop on paper.

day 67

sometimes,
i catch myself looking for you in a crowd.

a habit i can't seem to break.

day 68

i noticed something today
the pain, it's a piece of me now
and in a weird way
i'm scared to let it go
because it feels like
it's the *last bit of you* i have
and if i lose that
will there be anything left
of *'us'* at all?

day 69

there's a sadness in me that even time can't heal.

day 70

every love song
now feels like
a personal attack.

the lyrics,
a reminder of a love
that's no more.

day 71

i'm learning to live with the void.

it's not about filling it,
but about accepting it as a part of my new self.

day 72

today, i caught myself not thinking about you
for a moment.

it was brief,
but in that moment, i saw a glimpse of a future
where i can breathe again.

day 73

maybe we were too happy and the evil eye got us

day 74

i feel stuck between
wanting to remember every detail about you and
wishing i could forget you completely.

day 75

i'm starting to accept that
some wounds don't completely heal.

they scar, and
you simply learn to live with them.

day 76

i whispered a goodbye to you tonight.
not sure if it's the first of many or the last.
only time will tell.

day 77

today, i find myself again whispering,
"i still love you"
it's like a song my heart refuses to stop singing.

i miss you in every quiet moment, every loud one.
i want to be with you, to be yours again.

day 78

i found a piece of your jewelry.
holding it felt like holding a piece of a lost treasure,
precious and painful.

day 79

sometimes i talk to you in my mind,
telling you about my day, my fears, my hopes.
it's like you never left.

i miss being yours.

day 80

i miss us,
the way we used to be,
perfectly in sync.

i want that back.
i want to be yours again.

day 81

i wonder if heartbreak ever truly leaves,
or if it just becomes a part of who you are.

day 82

i find pieces of you in everything i do.
in the quiet of the morning,
in the hustle of the day,
you're always there,
a constant presence in my heart.

day 83

the memories of us are bittersweet.

they bring both joy and pain,
but mostly,
they remind me of
how much i want to be with you again.

i love you, more than time can fade.

day 84

sometimes, i wonder if you feel this emptiness too.
do you think of me?
do you miss me?

day 85

i walked past our favorite spot today.
everything reminded me of you – of us.

i stood there,
wishing for a chance to start again,
to be the one you come home to.

day 86

in the delicate moonlit fabric of my dreams, your presence felt remarkably close, like a comforting sip of coffee in the quiet hours of night. the dream unfolded by the water's edge, where reflections danced beneath the lamplight's glow. yet, reality, like a belt tightening around my heart, returned with the dawn, leaving only the lingering essence of your memory in the bag of dreams i carry through each day.

day 87

i can't help but think about
how perfect we were together.

i keep hoping for a sign,
a chance to say i'm still yours,
that my heart belongs to you.

day 88

i saw your favorite book at the store
and it brought back so many memories.

i remember how you'd read to me.
i miss those days, i miss being yours.

day 89

i miss your laugh,
the way it made everything feel okay.

i'd give anything to be yours again.

day 90

three months without you. the pain is still there.
you're the one i want, the one i love.
i wish i could tell you i'm still yours.

day 91

i tried to do things we loved,
but they're not the same without you.

day 92

sometimes i just sit and look at our pictures,
remembering the good times.
it makes me wonder if there's still a chance for us.
i want to be with you, to be yours.

day 93

the nights are the hardest.
i lie awake thinking about you, about us.
i miss your warmth, your voice.

day 94

i saw something funny today and
my first thought was to share it with you.

day 95

every day, i hope you'll call,
that you'll say you miss me too.

day 96

i still wear the watch you gave me.
it's a reminder of the times we shared,
a hope that maybe, someday, i'll be yours again.

day 97

i went through our messages,
reliving each conversation.

day 98

i heard *our song* on the radio.
it took all my strength not to cry.
every lyric speaks of you, of us.

i wish we could go back to those days,
to being in love.

day 99

another day without you.
the desire to be with you, to be yours, hasn't faded.

it's a constant yearning, a hope that maybe,
in another tomorrow,
we can find our way back to each other.

day 100

it's a milestone i never wanted to reach
a hundred days of waking up to a world
that's a little less bright
without you in it

the laughter, the tears, the love we shared
now they're just echoes
echoes that fill the rooms where we once made plans
dreams that have long since faded

but still, i count
because with each number, i remember
one hundred moments,
one hundred breaths,
one hundred whispers of your name

and i wonder if you ever whisper mine too

day 101

today,
i wore the sweater you loved on me.

it's like a hug from you,
one i long for but can't have.

day 102

more than a hundred days without you.
each day feels like a page in a book where the story
ended too soon.

day 103

we were so happy
but i don't know wtf happened

day 104

i heard someone laugh like you today.
my heart raced,
only to crash when i realized it wasn't you.

day 105

the emptiness is overwhelming.
i never knew silence could be so loud.

day 106

i find myself talking to your photo.
it's a one-sided conversation, but it's all i have.

day 107

you should read the "notes" in my phone
i have written a lot about you

day 108

i saw a couple in love and felt a pang of jealousy.
they have what we lost.

day 109

your absence feels like a wound that won't heal,
a scar that won't fade.

day 110

i wonder if you ever think of me.
does my memory haunt you like yours does me?

day 111

i still save two cups of coffee in the morning,
out of habit,
hoping somehow you'd be there to drink it.

day 112

i can't delete our messages.
they're the last pieces of you i have.

day 113

your favorite song played on the radio.
i had to pull over, the tears wouldn't stop.

day 114

i look for you in every crowd, in every face.
it's a fruitless search, but i can't help myself.

day 115

i dreamt of you again.
waking up to your absence is a cruel reality.

day 116

i keep replaying our last moments together,
wondering where it all went wrong.

day 117

can we do just one more phone call?
i really wanna know how are you doing?

day 118

i miss the way you looked at me,
as if i was your entire world.

day 119

i still cook your favorite meal,
hoping somehow the aroma will bring you back.

day 120

yes, i still cry
i still cry a lot thinking of you

day 121

every love story i hear reminds me of ours,
and how ours didn't have a happy ending.

day 122

i still write you texts i'll never send.
it's my way of keeping our conversation alive.

day 123

i saw your name in a book
and my heart skipped a beat,
as if the mere mention could bring you back.

day 124

that last kiss
i didn't know
it was our goodbye
if i had known
i would've held on
a little longer

tried to memorize
how it felt
'cause now
i'd give anything
for one more
just one more kiss

day 125

i lit a candle for us tonight.
a small flame to keep the memory of our love alive.

day 126

what you're doing at this very moment.
are you thinking of me too?

day 127

i've been going to bed early these days.
you know, i only sleep early when i'm feeling sad.

day 128

i walked by your office building today,
half-hoping, half-fearing i might see you.

day 129

i can't bring myself to watch our favorite movie.
it doesn't feel right *without you.*

day 130

i miss the way you made me feel,
like i was the most important person in the world.

day 131

your number is still labelled as "babe" in my phone

day 132

i miss our late night calls
i miss you so bad

day 133

i keep asking why.
why did we end?
why can't i move on?
why does it still hurt so much?

day 134

your smell is fading from the pillows.
i'm losing you all over again.

day 135

i watched the sunset alone,
wishing you were here to share the beauty.

day 136

i still reach for my phone to text you.

day 137

i visit places we used to go,
hoping to feel closer to you,
but it only amplifies your absence.

day 138

i find myself pausing at things you would have liked.
a book, a song, a joke. it's like you're still here,
but just out of reach.

day 139

omg! how childish we were,
remember those
'i love you',
'i love you too',
'i love you 3',
'i love you 4'.....

day 140

i heard someone call *your name* today.
for a moment, my world stopped, hoping it was you.

day 141

i wonder
if you still remember the promises we made,
the dreams we shared.

day 142

i still have your number memorized.
it's a number i'll never call, but can't forget.

day 143

i miss your touch, i miss your warmth.

day 144

i remember the times
you'd say: "you're being silly";
i'd hug you tight
our little fights
were just another way
to say "i'm here"
and "i won't go away"

day 145

in my sleep, we're still happy, still together.

day 146

i passed by our old hangout spot.
it's changed, just like us.

day 147

i find comfort in our memories,
but it's a comfort that's lined with pain.

day 148

i still have your texts.
sometimes,
i read them just to hear your voice in my head.

day 149

i wonder if you ever regret us ending.
do you ever think about what could have been?

day 150

babe, i'm losing contact with everyone,
and i'm feeling so alone.

day 151

that first smile
it's always in my mind
like it was just yesterday
you looked at me
and the world
just lit up

day 152

i keep hoping to run into you,
just to see your face,
even if it's just for a second.

day 153

i still want to send memes to you

i still find funny things
and my first thought is you
i want to send them
share a laugh
like we used to

day 154

you know coffee still tastes good,
but it was much better with you.

day 155

i saw someone wearing your style of clothes.
my heart raced, only to be disappointed.

day 156

i wonder if you kept the things i gave you.
are they as precious to you as yours are to me?

day 157

i saw your favorite car today.
for a moment, i thought it was you driving.

day 158

i tried to visit our favorite spot by the lake.
the memories were too strong, too painful.

day 159

i keep thinking about the trips we planned.
now, they're just dreams that will never come true.

day 160

i heard a song that described us perfectly.
it felt like it was written just for us.
should i send it you?

day 161

i keep thinking about
what i would say if i saw you again.

there's so much left unsaid.

day 162

i wish we could talk again in 2024

day 163

i still remember your favorite coffee order.
it's a small detail, but it means everything.

day 164

i saw a photo of us pop up in my memories.
we looked so happy, so in love.

day 165

i keep hoping you'll call,
even though i know you won't.

day 166

no one,
literally no one, knows how much i cried that day.

day 167

i still have our plans written in my planner.
it's hard to erase them, like i'm erasing our future.

day 168

remember how you used to make fun of my nose
turning red whenever i got angry?

day 169

we never really fought
it was like a game
every time
we'd end up smiling
i miss playing
that game with you

day 170

you were mine
i was yours

and oh, how sweet it was

day 171

i wonder if you still wear the watch i gave you.
does it remind you of me, like yours does to me?

day 172

i walked through our neighborhood.
every corner, every street holds a memory of us.

day 173

in the quiet moments of reflection, like a clock ticking steadily, i find myself yearning for the days when your genuine interest in me illuminated our connection. your curiosity, a beacon brighter than stars in the night sky, was a comforting presence, casting light on every shared moment. i miss the depth of our conversations, the way your attention fluttered around the details of my life like birds in flight. now, that interest has become a memory—a vibrant thread that once wove through our moments, like clouds drifting across the sky. in the hushed spaces of solitude, i feel the absence of your inquisitive spirit, a void where your genuine fascination used to reside, much like a message in a bottle lost at sea.

day 174

when you got mad
i'd make funny faces
just to see you smile
i wish i could do that now
to see that smile
just once more

day 175

you were my moon

day 176

i found a note you left me once.
your handwriting brought back a flood of emotions.

day 177

i heard your name in a conversation,
and omg, believe me, i almost cried.

day 178

i keep hoping for a sign from you, a message, a call.
anything to know i still mean something to you.

day 179

i miss those screenshots we took
during our facetime calls.

day 180

it's been six months now
the "really bad hurting" has gotten a bit quieter

but the "missing you part"
that hasn't gone anywhere

it's like having this quiet hum
in the background
all the time
just there, you know?

day 181

it's my birthday
and i keep glancing at the phone
half-expecting
you might remember
and drop a call or a text
part of me knows
it's just a wish
but still
i hope

day 182

i deserved a better goodbye
maybe one last hug too?

day 183

you left, you just left
you didn't utter a word
maybe you could have told me that you are leaving

day 184

you said you won't leave
then why did you?

day 185

you knew me
knew me so well
inside out, every piece
you saw it all
and still
you chose to leave

day 186

i miss you, the old you
yes, the one that's not there anymore

day 187

i heard our song today.
it used to make us dance, now it just makes me cry.

day 188

you know what?
even now a hug could resolve everything.

day 189

i saw a couple laughing, and for a moment,
i remembered what happiness feels like.

day 190

i still remember the way you made me feel.
it's a feeling i haven't found since you left.

day 191

if i send a text saying *'i miss you'*
can we start again?
or would you even reply?

day 192

i keep hoping you'll come back,
even though i know deep down, you won't.

day 193

i tried to go to that favorite karaoke place,
but it felt wrong without you.

day 194

i miss your kisses. i miss your love.

day 195

i saw your favorite band is in town.
remember how we always said
we'd go see them together?

day 196

i still want you
and i miss how badly you wanted me

day 197

i saw a shooting star and wished for you.
it's a childish wish, but i can't help it.

day 198

i tried to write a poem about you,
but the words wouldn't come.

it's like i'm lost for words without you.

day 199

i saw your favorite flower today.
it reminded me of the bouquets you used to give me.

day 200

it's weird to think
i've woken up two hundred times
and you weren't there
not even one of those days
the world's kept spinning
and i've been doing all those life things
you know, like groceries and laundry
but there's this space
where you used to be
and it's like i can almost hear it
sometimes i'll be doing something totally normal
and it'll hit me
that you're not around
and it's like this quiet part of the room
just gets louder
i've got so many things i want to tell you
like how i finally tried that spicy ramen place
or how the neighbor's cat had kittens
small stuff, but stuff i'd usually tell you
and on days like today
it just builds up
like a story i can't tell
'cause the person who should hear it
isn't here to listen
two hundred days
and i'm still talking to you in my head
still missing you
isn't that something?

day 201

i am so tired.
idk i just feel so numb.
so lost in your thoughts babe.

day 202

in the quiet wishes of my heart, i really want to go back
in time. not to change anything, but to live those
wonderful moments again.
the laughter, the warmth, and all those special times
that made life beautiful—i wish i could experience
them once more. it's not about regret; it's about
relishing the magic of those moments that still sparkle
in my memories.

day 203

learning to be alone again is hard. every morning, i check my phone, hoping for a text from you, but it never comes. the routines we shared are now just mine, and it feels lonely. being alone is tough, and each day is like a new struggle. i miss our time together, and it's not easy to forget. i'm trying to get used to being by myself, but it's really emotional, and *i wish things were different.*

day 204

i still think about the words i would say if i could talk
to you one more time.

so much left unsaid.

day 205

i saw a couple celebrating their anniversary.
it reminded me of the *future* we'll never have.

day 206

i found an old gift from you. it's amazing how
something so small can hold so much meaning.

day 207

i tried cooking your favorite recipe.
the taste brought back a flood of memories,
sweet and painful.

day 208

i still visit the cafe where we used to go.
your ghost sits across from me,
sipping coffee in silence.

day 209

you left,
now i'm searching,
for you,
and my lost smile.

day 210

i still sleep on my side of the bed, leaving your side untouched, as if waiting for you to return.

day 211

i found a message from you i never replied to.
it's too late now.

day 212

in the evocative strains of a song, i discovered the poignant retelling of our story. the melody wove through the air, each note resonating with the depth of our shared experiences. the lyrics, like a lyrical archaeologist, unearthed emotions long buried, cutting through the layers of time with precision. as the music played, it became a storyteller, narrating the chapters of our past with haunting clarity.
the song became a vessel, carrying the echoes of what was lost, and in its embrace, i found the bittersweet beauty of reminiscence.

day 213

i tried to visit our favorite park,
but every bench,
every tree
whispered memories of you.

day 214

my morning routine is still the same.
i wake up and check my phone
just to see if you texted me,
but there never is.

day 215

i keep thinking about the plans we made,
dreams now gathering dust
in the corners of my mind.

day 216

today,
i missed you a bit more than usual.

i wanted to talk to you,
even though i know you don't want to.

when i realized i couldn't call you, i
just started to cry—cry a lot, cry out loud.

i don't know why,
but your face was there in front of me.
i couldn't do anything but cry.

i miss you so much.
i really, really loved you with all my heart.
i don't understand why we didn't end up together.
we were way too perfect to be apart.

day 217

i still have the pictures we took.
we were so much in love.

day 218

wherever you are, i really wish you are happy.
wherever you are, i really wish you are happy.
wherever you are, i really wish you are happy.
wherever you are, i really wish you are happy.
wherever you are, i really wish you are happy.
wherever you are, i really wish you are happy.
wherever you are, i really wish you are happy.
wherever you are, i really wish you are happy.
wherever you are, i really wish you are happy.
wherever you are, i really wish you are happy.
wherever you are, i really wish you are happy.
wherever you are, i really wish you are happy.
wherever you are, i really wish you are happy.
wherever you are, i really wish you are happy.
wherever you are, i really wish you are happy.
wherever you are, i really wish you are happy.
wherever you are, i really wish you are happy.
wherever you are, i really wish you are happy.
wherever you are, i really wish you are happy.
wherever you are, i really wish you are happy.
wherever you are, i really wish you are happy.
wherever you are, i really wish you are happy.
wherever you are, i really wish you are happy.
wherever you are, i really wish you are happy.
wherever you are, i really wish you are happy.
wherever you are, i really wish you are happy.
wherever you are, i really wish you are happy.
wherever you are, i really wish you are happy.

day 219

i keep your messages saved.

sometimes, reading them is the only way
to hear your voice again.

day 220

i visited the beach we loved.
the waves echoed my longing,
a rhythmic reminder of you.

day 221

just one of those days,
can't shake your face from my mind.

day 222

heard our song on the radio
took all my strength not to call

day 223

i went through our photos on my phone today.
your face,
your smile,
it's digital but
it's all i have.

every pixel is a memory,
every memory a sharp joy.

day 224

missed your goodnight text
the night just isn't the same

day 225

it's getting colder now.
i wear the scarf you knitted for me,
wrap myself in it like a hug.

it's not enough, but it's something.

day 226

another day down
they say time heals but when

day 227

wanted to share good news with you
forgot i couldn't, hurts every time

day 228

someone said my smile looks like yours
wish i could see yours *again*

day 229

it's weird not knowing how your day went
guess i'll never know now

day 230

i laughed today, first time in ages
wished you were here to hear it

day 231

it rained, and i hoped you were dry
old habits die hard

day 232

went to a party.
people there, they were strangers,
not our kind of crowd.
i felt out of place without you,
like a lost child in a busy market.

day 233

your book is still where you left it
can't bring myself to move it

day 234

people say, i look better
they don't know i'm faking it

day 235

i cooked dinner for one tonight.
it was quiet, too quiet.

i miss our kitchen dances,
the laughter,
the warmth of your body close to mine.

day 236

a friend asked how i've been.
"i'm getting by," i said.

but the truth is,
i'm a ship lost at sea,
you were my anchor babe.

day 237

i tried not to
but again, i read some old messages from you.

it's a double-edged sword, comfort, and pain all at
once. i can hear your voice in every word.

day 238

someone asked about you today, babe
i changed the subject

day 239

i write these notes to you every night
it's like sending messages to the stars

day 240

i'm trying to find new hobbies
but nothing's as fun without you

day 241

work was tough today.
came home wishing i could tell you about it.
you always knew what to say to make it better.

day 242

the nights are the longest
missing your voice in the dark

day 243

i almost dialed your number
by muscle memory alone

day 244

saw two birds outside my window
reminded me of us, free

day 245

the coffee tastes bitter
without you here to share it, babe.
i remember
how you'd complain if i made it too strong.

day 246

the leaves are changing colors
wish we could walk through them together

day 247

i'm learning to live with the silence
but sometimes it's too loud

day 248

i still tell you "good morning"
though i know you can't hear

day 249

i helped someone today
you always said it'd make me feel better

day 250

a quarter of a thousand days
you're still my first thought every morning

day 251

it's your birthday
the first since you've been gone
i miss planning our little party
i thought about sending a gift
i still remember where you live
should i?

day 252

my friends asked about you today.
did yours ask about me too?
if they did, did you tell them
that you were the one who left?

day 253

i miss you so much and with every passing hour, i miss you even more… and more *and i really wish you were here.*

day 254

"eu sinto sua falta"
"mi manchi"
"ich vermisse dich"

different languages, same meaning;
"i miss you"

day 255

hoped to see you again,
even if just a glimpse from afar.

day 256

heard our song.
it's no longer ours, just a melody of a past love.

day 257

i saw your favorite candy at the store today.
bought it without thinking.
now it's sitting on the counter, untouched.

day 258

it's your favorite team's game night, babe.
i almost texted you to come over.

day 259

your side of the closet remains untouched,
a tribute to our happier times.

day 260

i tried that new restaurant downtown,
the one we were excited about.

it wasn't the same without you across the table.

day 261

again, there was a shooting star tonight, babe.
i made a wish for you, wherever you are.
i really wish you stay happy.

day 262

i found an old grocery list we made together.
your handwriting next to mine.

it's the little things that hit the hardest.

day 263

there's a new show on netflix
we would have binged, babe.

can't bring myself to watch it.

day 264

washed the car today
and found your sunglasses.

they're on the dashboard,
like you just left them there.

day 265

i listened to your voicemail again, babe.
just to hear your voice.

day 266

i do talk to a number of people,
get distracted for awhile
but again
it's just me and your thoughts
and all the flashbacks

can't stop thinking about you
thinking about the time we spent together

day 267

i've never cried like this in my life ever,
escaping from my friends,
going to my room and crying for some time,
doing it again and again.

this hurts really bad.

i wish we could have ended up together
because since you left,
nothing feels right.

day 268

and sometimes i just miss you a bit more
and can't help myself
can't stop myself from crying

day 269

i miss you
i miss your texts
i miss your voice

i miss the way you used to share everything that's
happening around the world

i miss the way we used to laugh together, sometimes
even on the serious things

i should have listened to you, when you said that we
might not have much time left together

day 270

i know you'll never read this

i loved you from all my heart
i thought we gonna be together forever
i never slept without thinking about you
i trusted you with everything
i never knew that you will break me
and i didn't know that you'll walk away so easily

day 271

your replies became dry
and you changed all of a sudden
but you know,
i still remember that sweet person
who used to look at me and smile.

day 272

i really needed one last hug from you

day 273

i still can't believe that you can live without me
because here, *i am dying*

dying to just listen to you voice one more time

day 274

what if we just start again?

day 275

i try to keep myself busy
by doing one thing or other
but
whenever there's a spare second
i start to think about you in that little moment

day 276

i remember the times
you'd shake your head
i'd just grin

soon we'd forget
why we were fussing
and just start laughing

day 277

remember
you'd be mad
i'd just smile
we both knew
our love was strong
it could take a little storm

day 278

remember the pair of shoes that you gifted me?
the one you liked the most!
ahh…. they are still safe in my closet.

day 279

people around you are so lucky,
they get to see you daily.

day 280

you
deserved
so much more,
and i wish i had
spent more time with you.
i hope you know how much i love you
and how much i miss you every day.

day 281

i owe you a lot

i started this journey with you
and now

now you aren't here
and i'm all alone
idk how to make decisions
you always helped me in choosing
and always just wished for my best

but with you gone
idk what to do
how to get back to normal

day 282

i watched the sunrise alone, babe.

remember
when
we
used
to
count
the
colors
together?

day 283

i found a sock of yours under the bed.
it's funny the things that can make your heart ache.

day 284

i cleared out a drawer for my new gym clothes, babe.

found one of your scarves.
kept it beside me all day.

day 285

the book you recommended?
i finally finished it, babe.

i get why you liked it so much.

day 286

i'm learning to play the guitar.
it's hard, but it's a distraction.

day 287

had a dream where you were a stranger.
maybe my heart is starting to let go.

day 288

i said your name out loud today, babe.
            just to break the silence.

day 289

i painted the living room.
it's a fresh start,
or at least it feels like one.

day 290

i donated some of your clothes, babe.
it was time, and it felt okay.

day 291

i'm cooking new recipes.
no more of our usual.
it's time for new tastes.

day 292

i laughed today, babe.
a real, genuine *laugh*.
it was surprising.

day 293

i went out with friends, babe.
i stayed the whole night and it was actually fun.

day 294

i'm volunteering at the shelter.
helping others feels good.

day 295

i'm ready to meet new people, babe.
it's a big step, but i'm taking it.

day 296

i'm reading again.
books you never heard of,
stories *just for me.*

day 297

walking alone

i realized
it's not that tough

day 298

i'm not waiting for you to come back anymore.
i'm moving forward.

day 299

i'm learning to be just me again, babe. not half of us.

day 300

it's a milestone.
i'm still here,
i'm still me,
and it's okay.

day 301

i laughed with a stranger today.
it was a brief moment of connection.

day 302

i'm picking up new hobbies, babe.
life's too short not to try.

day 303

i'm making peace with your absence.
it's a quiet kind of acceptance.

day 304

i'm no longer checking my phone for you, babe.

day 305

i'm singing in the shower again.
it's been a while.
it feels good.

day 306

woke up to the sound of rain tapping against the window. instead of staying in bed, i put on my jacket and went for a walk. the rain felt cleansing, washing away the lingering doubts, leaving me refreshed and a little more ready to face the world.

day 307

there's a new coffee blend at the shop.
i tried it on a whim and loved it.
it's a new favorite,
something that's just mine,
not shared, not a compromise.

day 308

i'm okay going to bed alone, babe.
the stars keep me company.

day 309

i'm not erasing you, babe. just writing a new chapter.

day 310

i'm okay with silence now.
it's filled with new beginnings.

day 311

i found a smile creeping on my face as i watched a
couple teach their daughter to ride a bike. their
happiness was infectious, and for once, i didn't spiral
into our 'what could have been'. i just enjoyed the
moment for what it was.

day 312

i'm embracing change.
it's not easy, but it's growth.

day 313

a memory popped up on my social media from years ago. instead of deleting it, i let it stay. it's a part of my history, after all, and i'm learning that history doesn't have to be painful.

day 314

i'm finding joy in little things, babe.
like the first snowfall of the season.

day 315

i'm okay with our memories.
they're *sweet*, not bitter.

day 316

i'm letting myself be happy, babe.
it's what you would have wanted.

day 317

i spent the evening star-gazing. the vastness of the night sky put things into perspective. my pain is just a tiny blip in the grand scheme of things, and somehow, that's comforting.

day 318

i'm appreciating new friendships.
life's bringing new people in.

day 319

went for a hike in the hills today. the fresh air, the silence except for the wind and birds, it was liberating. i felt like i could breathe deeply for the first time in months.

day 320

i tried
a new recipe
for dinner,
and it turned out great.

it's nice to know
that i can still surprise myself,
that there are successes
waiting for me in new experiences.

day 321

thought about our unfulfilled plans. they're no longer
regrets, but steps towards the person i'm becoming.

day 322

found an old message from you.
it's a voice from the past,
but my present is louder and more colorful.

day 323

i'm noticing more laughter in my days. at work, with friends, even alone with a funny video. laughter used to remind me of you, but now it's just a part of my day, and that's a big step.

day 324

the plants
you left behind
are thriving.

i've taken to talking to them
as i water them.

it's my new routine,
and they're my new silent companions
in this journey.

day 325

i'm not sad about our ending, babe.
it was just the start of something new for me.

day 326

i joined a local community group.
meeting new people,
sharing ideas
and working on projects, i
t's all helping me rebuild
a sense of community that i didn't realize i'd lost.

day 327

i've started to enjoy the solitude of my evening walks.
there's a peace in the rhythm of my steps and the quiet
of the streets. it's a time for me to gather my thoughts
and appreciate the calm.

day 328

i'm not rushing to fill the silence with noise anymore.

there's a music in the quiet
that i'm starting to appreciate,
a tune that's all my own.

day 329

there's a new plant on my desk, a resilient little
cactus. it's tough and a bit prickly, much like i've
had to be. but it's thriving, and that gives me hope.

day 330

walked through our park.

the memories are there,
but
they're accompanied by a sense of tranquility
and acceptance.

day 331

i decided to learn how to make bread from scratch. the process was messy and imperfect, much like the way i've been handling things. but the end result was delicious— a perfect metaphor for this messy, beautiful life.

day 332

i laughed so hard today
my sides hurt.

it was a reminder that joy can be found
in the simplest moments,
and it's okay to let it in.

day 333

i baked a cake today, just because i wanted to. it's
liberating, doing things just for myself, not because
it's a tradition or a shared joy, but simply a personal
pleasure.

day 334

today,
i went back
to that little café we loved.

it's under new management,
and it's different now.
so am i.

i enjoyed a cup of coffee
and left feeling surprisingly refreshed.

day 335

i accepted a dinner invitation tonight.
no expectations,
no pressure,
just an evening out.

it was delightful.

day 336

i've taken to writing,
not just journal entries, but stories.

it's a way to channel all these emotions into
something beautiful,
something lasting.

day 337

i'm learning
that it's okay to look back,
as long as i don't forget to turn back around
and keep moving forward.

day 338

there's a new series
i've started watching.

it's not usually what i'd choose,
but i'm finding joy in the unexpected.

day 339

i'm starting to think about the future more,
about travel plans,
career moves,
life changes.

there's an entire world out there waiting for me.

day 340

i've begun to let go of the guilt of moving on.
it's not a betrayal, it's a necessity. and it's healthy.

day 341

i'm okay with our story ending, babe.
every book has a last page.

day 342

i'm making peace
with the idea that our paths have diverged.
it's not with a heavy heart, but with a hopeful spirit.

day 343

i'm not searching for your replacement.
i'm building a new life.

day 344

i've realized that
i can cherish our past without living in it.

there's a difference, and it's an important one.

day 345

today, i found myself giving advice to a friend going
through a tough time.
i sounded like you, babe, and it made me smile.

day 346

i finally
opened the box of mementos
i've kept hidden away.

letters, tickets, pictures...
i thought
it would break me,
but
it didn't.

each item
told a story of us,
and i'm finally at a place
where i can be grateful
for those stories.

day 347

i'm starting to redefine what happiness means to me.
it's not a *shared* concept anymore,
it's uniquely mine.

day 348

i'm okay with moving on, babe.
it doesn't mean i've forgotten, just that i'm ready.

day 349

i'm okay with saying this, babe.

i loved you, i miss you,
but
i'm ready for a new chapter.

day 350

i'm learning that healing isn't linear, babe.
it's a series of spirals, and i'm on the upward curve.

day 351

slept on my side of the bed.
the other side is no longer a void,
but a space for new dreams and possibilities.

day 352

just remember that i am so proud of you

day 353

returned to our special place.
it's different now, just as i am,
reflecting the changes time brings.

day 354

i'm finding that i can be both strong and soft.
it's not one or the other.

day 355

saw a couple
sharing a meal.

it reminded me
of us
but
also filled me
with hope
for
new connections.

day 356

i'm learning to trust the journey.

trust myself,
trust life.

day 357

i'm okay with growth.
it's been tough, but i'm blooming.

day 358

today,
i sat by the river,
watching the water flow.

it's a metaphor for life,
i suppose.

always moving,
always changing,
and
i'm learning to move with it.

day 359

i'm discovering that i can be my own best friend.

day 360

i find myself in a realm beyond the shadows of our shared moments. each passing day has carried me further from the echoes of what once was, but remnants persist—a silent tribute to the intricacies of our journey.

your birthday, a perennial marker on the calendar of recollections, stands vivid amidst the tapestry of my memories. the indelible imprints of our shared moments echo through time, resonating with the fragrance of the past that refuses to dissipate.

the recollection of our first meeting dances in the corridors of my mind, a vivid scene that unfolds with every reminiscent thought. it is a chapter of our history that time has not erased, a touchstone to the genesis of what became a complex narrative.

the mere utterance of your name acts as a catalyst, summoning flashbacks that play like scenes from a bygone era. it's a symphony of emotions, a kaleidoscope of images and feelings that surge forth with the mere invocation of your identity.

yes, i still miss you, a sentiment that lingers in the recesses of my heart. however, with the passage of time, the yearning transforms. the desire remains, but the wanting is tempered by the acknowledgment that our paths have diverged.

the memories persist, but the gravitational pull of your presence has diminished. what once bound me in an unspoken tether has now become a series of fading echoes. the ache subsides, gradually replaced by the ebb and flow of new experiences.

on day 360, i confront the paradox of missing someone yet choosing to release them. the heart retains its yearning, but the journey forward necessitates a letting go—a recognition that the path ahead is one of self-discovery and healing.

in the quiet spaces between the lines, the memories find solace. they exist not as shackles but as threads woven into the fabric of my story. the echoes persist, reverberating with the bittersweet melody of what once was—a testament to the complexity of navigating the aftermath of love.

day 361

i've started
to find beauty
in the little things
again.

a child's laughter,
a perfect cup of coffee,
a quiet evening.
it's a gift
to be able to appreciate
these moments.

day 362

a song came
on the radio
that used to be
'our' song.

i let it play this time,
singing along
to the lyrics.

it's becoming just a song again,
and that's okay.

day 363

now that we're not together, i don't want to be the cause of any more of your tears. i hope you find all the love and happiness you deserve. remember that you are an incredible person, and you have so much to offer the world. keep pushing forward, and never forget how amazing you truly are.

day 364

i'm okay with the story continuing, babe.
our chapter ended, but the book goes on.

day 365

as the final page of this chapter turns, i pause to reflect on the journey that has brought me here, to this pivotal moment of closure and rebirth. one full year has passed—a year measured not just in days, but in the breadth and depth of emotions that have coursed through me, each leaving their indelible mark.

in this orbit around the sun, i have come full circle. i have experienced love in its most intoxicating form, a love that lifted me to the highest peaks of joy and plunged me into the depths of despair in its loss. i have navigated the turbulent waters of grief, each wave a lesson, each lesson a stepping stone towards a newfound strength.

i've lost, not just a partner, but a piece of myself that i thought was indispensable. yet, in that loss, i've discovered the unyielding resilience of the human spirit—my spirit— that refuses to be quelled by sorrow. the pain, once a constant companion, has transformed. it has softened from a searing flame to a warm ember, a scar that no longer wounds but reminds me of the journey i have endured. it is a testament to survival, a badge of honor that speaks of battles fought and inner demons faced.

and now, i stand at the precipice of tomorrow, looking out at the horizon with eyes that see the world differently. the hurt hasn't disappeared; perhaps it never truly will. but it has been woven into the very essence of my being, a thread in the intricate tapestry of my life. it is a part of my story, but it is not the entirety of it.

i am okay. more than okay, i am at peace—a peace hard-earned and well-deserved. there is a certain tranquility in acceptance, in acknowledging the impermanence of all things and finding the courage to let go. my heart, once heavy with yearning, now beats with the promise of new beginnings.

the future awaits, a canvas stretched out before me, vast and untouched. i am ready to pick up the brush once more, to paint the next chapter of my life with bold strokes fueled by the wisdom gained from the past. i am ready to embrace the joys and challenges that await, to live fully and love deeply once more.

today marks the end of a significant passage in my life, but also the dawn of something new. it's day one of the rest of my life—a life that is uniquely mine, a life that i step into with an open heart and an unshakable resolve to make the most of every moment. the journey continues, and i with it, ever forward, ever upward.

stay connected :)

if this journey through "365 days after you" has resonated with you, i would be deeply grateful if you could take a moment to leave a review on *amazon*. your thoughts and reflections not only help others discover this story but also mean the world to me as an author.

i would also love to hear from you on social media! if you decide to share your thoughts or favorite quotes from the book, please tag me in your stories. it's always a joy to connect with readers and i look forward to resharing your insights and experiences.
together, we continue to grow and heal, and your voice is an important part of this continuing journey.

thank you for your support and for being a part of this story.

~ mr. den
  @poemsbyden
  @scrawled_diary

acknowledgements

looking back on the journey of writing this book, my heart
is filled with deep gratitude and love for each and every
one of you who have supported me along the way.
mum and dad, your love and unwavering support have
been the light that guided me through even the darkest
moments. to my dear siblings, you have been my constant
cheerleaders, encouraging me to keep going when the
going got tough.
my friends and loved ones, you have stood by my side
through thick and thin, offering your love, your strength,
and your unwavering support. i am forever grateful for the
laughs, the hugs, and the countless cups of tea that have
helped me along the way.
to those whom i have lost on this journey, your memory
and your spirit live on through these pages, inspiring me to
keep pushing forward and never give up on my dreams.
and to all of the incredible instagram poets out there, your
stunning work has been a source of inspiration and beauty
in my life, reminding me of the power of words and the
magic of creativity.
finally, to my dear readers, thank you for connecting with
me, for sharing your own stories and struggles, and for
supporting me in this journey. your words of
encouragement and your love have been the fuel that kept
me going. i am humbled and honored to have you in my
life.

i'm eternally grateful to you guys.

about the author

meet *mr. den*, an enigmatic writer and poet whose words possess the extraordinary ability to touch hearts and souls. with three previously published books, including "eyes scream," "embrace the timing," and "scrawled diary," mr. den has cultivated a dedicated following on platforms such as instagram and tiktok.

despite his growing fan base under the handles *@poemsbyden* and *@scrawled_diary*, mr. den chooses to remain anonymous, allowing his work to speak for itself.

in "365 days after you," a profound journey from loss to healing, mr. den delves into the depths of emotions, capturing the essence of love, heartbreak, and resilience.

when he's not crafting poignant verses,
mr. den finds inspiration in the beauty of nature during long drives and hikes.

get in touch with him on instagram and tiktok-
@poemsbyden

Printed in Great Britain
by Amazon